THE CURSE OF THE
TOMB ROBBERS

AN ANCIENT EGYPTIAN PUZZLE MYSTERY

ANDY SEED

JAMES WESTON LEWIS

For Isla and Etta – A.S.

For Mabli Clem, with all my love – J.W.L.

First published 2022 by Nosy Crow Ltd
The Crow's Nest, 14 Baden Place,
Crosby Row, London, SE1 1YW, UK

Nosy Crow Eireann Ltd
44 Orchard Grove, Kenmare,
Co Kerry, V93 FY22, Ireland

www.nosycrow.com

ISBN 978 1 83994 657 8 (HB)
ISBN 978 1 78800 965 2 (PB)

Nosy Crow and associated logos are trademarks
and/or registered trademarks of Nosy Crow Ltd.

Published in collaboration with the British Museum.
With special thanks to John Taylor at the British Museum for his contribution and advice.

Text © Andy Seed 2022
Illustrations © James Weston Lewis 2022

The right of Andy Seed to be identified as the author and James Weston Lewis
to be identified as the illustrator of this work has been asserted.

A CIP catalogue record for this book is available from the British Library.

Printed in China.
Papers used by Nosy Crow are made from wood
grown in sustainable forests.

1 3 5 7 9 8 6 4 2 (HB)
1 3 5 7 9 8 6 4 2 (PB)

CONTENTS

Introduction 4   IIII

Thieves in the Desert 6   III

A Marketplace Plot 10   ∩

In the House of Scribes 14   ∩IIII

A Message in the Vizier's Kitchen 18   ∩IIIII

Crossing the Nile 22   ∩∩II

The Embalming Rooms 24   ∩∩IIII

Objects for the Dead 28   ∩∩IIIIII

At the Wall of the Gods 30   ∩∩∩

The Mystery of the Pyramids 34   ∩∩∩IIII

Entering the Secret Passage 36   ∩∩∩IIIIII

Terror in the Burial Chamber 40   ∩∩∩∩

The End of the Curse? 42   ∩∩∩∩II

Puzzle Solutions 46   ∩∩∩∩IIIIII

Glossary 48   ∩∩∩∩IIIIIIII

INTRODUCTION

Welcome to ancient Egypt. The year is 1422 BC, and a terrible crime is about to unfold. Can you help apprentice scribe Nub and his friend Iteti to crack the code and stop the curse?

NUB

Nub is an apprentice scribe who has been learning how to read and write in hieroglyphs since he was just five years old. As an orphan, he both lives and studies at his scribe school. His favourite thing to do when he has time off from lessons is explore the city and the land around it, in search of adventure with his friend Iteti.

ITETI

The daughter of a vizier (an important official who advises the pharaoh), Iteti lives in a grand house close to the pharaoh's palace, where she is supposed to be learning how to take care of running the home. Her favourite thing to do when she can escape her servants' watchful gaze is to learn how to read and write in hieroglyphs, with the help of Nub.

CODEBREAKER

Nub and Iteti have to solve 11 puzzles on their adventure but can you crack the code and help them? The ancient Egyptians wrote in a mysterious picture language and this book will help you unlock its secrets. Follow the clues on each page and use the fold-out hieroglyph charts and dictionary at the back of the book to help you read the words of the pharaohs!

To read hieroglyphs you must first write down what each sign stands for in the Egyptian language by using the hieroglyph charts at the back of the book. Once you have spelled out an Egyptian word, flip the page over and use the dictionary to translate your word into English.

Here's an example:

PUZZLE
What does this Egyptian word written in hieroglyphs mean?

Finding each sign in the charts at the back of the book and writing it in letters, then translating them to English, we get this:

f

q

a

cake

You will need a pen and paper. Good luck!

OBSERVATION CHALLENGE
Can you spot the scorpion lurking in every scene?
There are also six cats hiding in the book.

THIEVES IN THE DESERT

"It's just SO hot here," said Nub, the desert sand burning under his bare feet.

"I know, but can't you feel how special this place is?" replied Iteti. "My father said that hundreds of important people are buried here – priests and scribes and palace officials."

"I'm not surprised they died, coming out here."

"Oi!" cried Iteti. "Don't make fun of the dead! They might be listening."

Nub was about to say sorry when he heard voices. Clambering to the top of the hill, the two friends peered from behind a rock. Across the narrow valley, a group of men were hurrying over the sand, carrying jars and decorated boxes.

"Are you thinking what I'm thinking?" asked Iteti.

"Tomb robbers!" whispered Nub, shaking with anger.

DID YOU KNOW?

The ancient Egyptians
believed that when a person
died, their spirit would travel to
a place called the underworld, where
they would have to pass a series of tests
to get into paradise. To help them on their
journey, the dead person's family would
bury useful objects with them, such
as furniture, precious jewels
and even food.

Nub and Iteti watched, horrified, as the men loaded their plunder on to two donkeys and headed out of the valley. But as the thieves left, Nub saw one of them drop a small scrap of papyrus.

Carefully, Nub and Iteti edged down into the valley and picked it up.

"Look, there's a message on it!" said Nub.

PUZZLE

What does the message on the scrap of papyrus say? It is written using signs called hieroglyphs. Use the guide at the back of the book to crack this ancient Egyptian code and discover the secret word the robbers left behind.

CODE CLUE

Many of the signs the ancient Egyptians used stand for sounds. In this case, each sign represents the sound of a letter.

A MARKETPLACE PLOT

That afternoon, Nub and Iteti went to the market, the only place they knew where there was a sycamore tree. Iteti glanced round and saw two of the robbers approaching.

"Quick, climb the tree!" she said.

They scrambled into the branches just in time. The heavily built men stood by the tree trunk, talking in low tones.

DID YOU KNOW?

There were no shops in ancient Egypt so the marketplace was always very busy. Stalls sold everything from fish and fruit to furniture, tools and clothes. Many people used bartering (swapping goods) although some paid with small pieces of silver or gold. Houses were made from mud bricks and were often so warm inside that people slept on the roof!

11

Among the thick leaves of the sycamore, Nub and Iteti listened in horror as the rest of the gang assembled and began to talk about their next robbery.

"They're going to raid the tomb of a queen!" whispered Iteti.

Nub's eyes were wide. With great care, he took out the wooden palette he always carried. He picked up a reed and dipped it in ink, then he began to make notes on a small piece of stone.

What will we find in this Queen Neith's tomb, then?

I'm told there are great riches: GOLD RINGS, BRACELETS and maybe even a valuable FALCON COLLAR.

"We must tell someone," said Iteti. "They're going to break into a grave and disturb the souls of the dead. This is terrible." Nub nodded. "We have to stop them."

PUZZLE

The robbers have mentioned three things they aim to steal from the queen's tomb. Nub has made notes of these using hieroglyphs. He also wrote another word they said. Can you spot the word that is not a piece of jewellery? Use the guide at the back of the book to decode the signs and solve the puzzle.

CODE CLUE

Scribes would add this sign at the end of a word to show a plural (more than one of something):

IN THE HOUSE OF SCRIBES

When the robbers finally left, Nub and Iteti raced to the nearby House of Scribes and found the master scribe Hori, a tall and serious man. He was holding a large scarab beetle charm, which he quickly dropped into a bag when the children arrived.

"Master, please, we have overheard something serious and terrible," gabbled Nub.

"Oh, it's you, boy. What do you want?"

"These men – cunning thieves – are plotting to break into the tomb of Queen Neith and steal her gold and jewels!"

Hori folded his arms. "Do you take me for a nincompoop? You expect me to believe this childish nonsense? It's pure imagination!"

Iteti's eyes were wide in disbelief but the sour-faced scribe turned away and waved an arm.

"Come on," said Nub, leading his friend away. "Let's find out where the queen's pyramid is. There is an inventory of tombs somewhere here."

Nub and Iteti walked into a large room full of old scrolls and papyrus records. But where would they find the right document?

Not here – this is a list of cat mummies.

When Nub began to read the inventory of tombs his face turned white.
"What's up?" said Iteti. "This is really not the place to be sick."

PUZZLE

Can you find the inventory of tombs using these clues?

- It's not grey or brown
- It's tied with dark string
- It's not horizontal
- It's in something square

And this is how to build a sphinx!

"I've found the location of Neith's burial place. It's across the Nile. But there is something else here. Her tomb is protected by a curse. It says, 'Whoever enters this place to make evil, may the crocodile and hippopotamus take them in water, may the snake and scorpion take them on land'."

"Ouch. Let's tell my father," said Iteti.

A MESSAGE IN THE VIZIER'S KITCHEN

"Where is my father?" Iteti asked a servant when they arrived at her house.

"I am sorry, but the vizier is away on important business, advising the pharaoh," replied the man.

Nub looked at Iteti and groaned. "What are we going to do now?"

"We must leave a message for my father to go to Queen Neith's tomb with soldiers, as soon as he returns," she whispered. "Then I think we should go there ourselves. We might be able to stop the robbers."

Nub nodded and began to look for a piece of pottery to write on. Iteti went into the kitchen to find some food for the journey. Senseneb, her father's most trusted servant, gave her bread, onions and dates.

When Nub brought the message, they gave it to Senseneb.
"This is really important," said Iteti. "Please give it to
my father the moment he returns."

Senseneb bowed. "Is something wrong?"
she said, but Nub and Iteti were already
rushing to the door and heading for the river,
knowing that there was no time to waste.

PUZZLE

Senseneb has realised that the children are heading into danger. She is desperate to read the message that Nub gave her, but servants were not taught to read and write. She cannot understand the whole message but there are two words that she thinks she can work out because they contain special signs that give clues to their meaning. Can you help her read the two words below? Use the guide at the back of the book to help you.

CODE CLUE

Not all hieroglyphs represent sounds. The Egyptians sometimes used meaning signs that show what a word might be, placed at the end of the word. For example, the word for frog is **krr** which has three sound signs plus a meaning sign, which is a picture of a frog:

Sound signs   Meaning sign

CROSSING THE NILE

The mighty River Nile stretched out before them, 500 metres wide and alive with activity. There were boats of all kinds, fishermen, traders carrying goods and people drawing water along the banks.

Nub asked a farmer collecting water with a shaduf where they could get a ferry across to the pyramids.

"Just there," said the man, pointing at a wooden jetty. "But you'll have to pay for it."

Why are we going into the reeds again?

PUZZLE

There is only one safe route across the river for Nub and Iteti's little boat. Can you find it? Can you also spot the two mischievous stowaway monkeys?

Yikes! Which way do we go, Nub?

Iteti looked at the bracelets on her arm. "I could trade some of my jewellery?"

"Phew, good idea," replied Nub. "It's better than half an onion."

Soon they were on the windy river in a small wooden boat.

The two friends were thinking the same thing: would they cross safely and what would they do if they caught up with the gang?

Careful, that crocodile is HUNGRY!

DID YOU KNOW?

The River Nile was remarkably important to the ancient Egyptians. It brought them food by watering and enriching the farmland, allowed trade with other people, made travel easier and provided fish and water all year round. It did have its dangers: strong currents, floods, hippos and child-eating crocodiles!

THE EMBALMING ROOMS

On the other side of the river, Nub and Iteti spotted a group of men entering a large stone building. Could it be the gang? The two friends followed.

"What is this place?" said Iteti when they reached the entrance.

Nub read the hieroglyphs painted around the door. "They're embalming rooms, where priests prepare bodies for the afterlife."

"Oh, are we allowed in there? Isn't it going to be full of blood and guts?"

"Maybe the gang went in to hide. We should be brave and follow them," said Nub, trying not to tremble.

The smell inside the embalming rooms was overpowering: a mixture of rotting flesh, incense and sweat. They couldn't see the robbers anywhere, but had they left behind a clue?

DID YOU KNOW?

Ancient Egyptians believed
that a dead person's spirit would
travel to the afterlife, so they
prepared the body to take the spirit on
this journey. Poorer people were buried in
the desert sand but for pharaohs, important
officials and the wealthy, special priests
preserved their bodies by turning them
into bandaged mummies and placing
them in decorated coffins.

At the end of the room, three men were adding amulets among the bandages they used to wrap a mummy.

"What do you children want?" barked a priest.

"I'm an apprentice scribe," said Nub. "We've been, er, told to practise reading the signs on, erm, coffins."

"Over there," said the priest, pointing. "But don't be long."

Two shadowy figures were already studying one of the coffins. They slipped away through a door when the children approached.

"Those must be the thieves," said Nub. "But what were they doing here?"

"The leader was pointing at this coffin," replied Iteti. "I think it belongs to someone important."

Nub studied it. "You're right. I bet they are planning whose tomb to rob next!"

PUZZLE

Do you think the children are right? What word has Iteti spotted?
Look at the section of the coffin lid below.
Again, the guide at the back of the book will help.

CODE CLUE

Hieroglyphs can be read in three different directions: from left to right, from right to left or even downwards. You can tell which way to read from the direction that the signs of people, animals or birds are facing. They always face towards the start – so in other words, you always read towards the face.

OBJECTS FOR THE DEAD

Iteti opened the door that the robbers had used to escape.

"Come on," she said. "We've got to stop them disturbing the dead queen and robbing other tombs."
Nub followed her, and the pair found themselves in a room full of objects, large and small, guarded by three burly soldiers. There were pots, jars, paintings, cups, trumpets, clothes, games, charms and more. A glint of gold revealed jewels, bracelets and precious necklaces.

"Whoa," gasped Nub. "There's fancy food as well – it's making my belly rumble."
Two servants were moving a heavy wooden chest bearing the eye of Horus.

"What are these things for?" Iteti asked one of them.
"A noble died recently. These are his belongings, for his tomb."

The friends looked around, their eyes wide at the riches about to be buried.

"No wonder the robbers came here," said Nub. "They're probably planning to steal all this later."

"But where are they?" said Iteti looking round. "They must have gone through one of these doors."

PUZZLE

The robbers have knocked a clay tile from the door they went through. Iteti finds the broken pieces and puts them together to make the right shape. The pieces are shown below. Can you work out which door the robbers went through? It will help to trace the pieces and cut them out.

AT THE WALL OF THE GODS

Nub and Iteti went through the door and found themselves outside. There was no sign of the gang except for a cloud of dust to the north. Beyond it they could make out the shapes of pyramids.

"Well, that's the way to go," said Iteti.

Nub threw up his arms. "We'll never catch up with them. We may as well go home. My feet are killing me, and I have a blister like a baboon's bottom."

The pyramids are giant tombs for royal rulers, built over 4,000 years ago. The largest is 140 metres high, contains over two million blocks of stone and took thousands of workers 20 years to construct. Later pharaohs chose to be buried in tombs cut into the solid rock of steep mountain valleys.

Iteti stomped her foot. "No way are we going home. We've come this far, and anyway, we have a duty to the dead. Have you forgotten you're an orphan? And my mother passed from this life too. I would hate to see her grave destroyed by wicked thieves and her afterlife spoiled!"

Nub nodded. She was right.

Iteti and Nub walked on and after an hour came to one of the great stone temples the pharaohs had built. It was covered in huge carvings of gods.

"Perhaps we should ask the gods for help?" said Nub.

"Yes, good idea," said Iteti. "But which is which?"

"There are words to describe each god written below. I'll show you how to read them."

PUZZLE

Nub tells Iteti that the four gods on the wall are:

1. Ra, the sun god.
2. Anubis, god of embalming and funerals.
3. Horus, god of the sky and kings.
4. Hathor, goddess of dancing and music.

He picks out the words written in the box under each god and helps Iteti read them. Can you decode each word to find out which god is which?

CODE CLUE

Scribes did not write each sign in a line like we write letters. They liked to fill up spaces neatly and so sometimes they put one hieroglyph under another in a word. You read these from top to bottom. For example, the word for bird, **apd**, is usually written like this:

THE MYSTERY OF THE PYRAMIDS

It was late afternoon when Nub and Iteti finally reached the pyramids. But there were so many! Some were huge with smooth, light stone glistening in the sun, while others were small, or old and crumbling.

"Which one is Queen Neith's?" asked Iteti.

"I have no idea," said Nub. "There must be someone we can ask."

Suddenly, Nub spotted a tall stone obelisk covered in hieroglyphs.

"Ah, this seems to be some kind of signpost to the pyramids. It has the names of pharaohs and queens and lots of numbers."

Iteti tried to make sense of it. "What do the numbers mean?"

"I think it's the number of paces to each pyramid from here."

"Yes, here is Queen Neith's name!"

Iteti jumped up and down with excitement. "What does it say?"

PUZZLE

Help Nub to read what the obelisk says. The number of paces to Queen Neith's pyramid is shown next to her name. What number is it?

CODE CLUE

In ancient Egypt, royal names were written inside a special shape called a 'cartouche'. Here is Queen Neith's name:

CODE CLUE

The ancient Egyptians had their own number system.
The following signs were used to show numbers.

VALUE	1	10	100	1,000	10,000	100,000	1,000,000
HIEROGLYPH						or	

These were put together to make any number, for example:

5 is shown as

32 is shown as

2,146 is shown as

The tombs of pharaohs and queens contained incredible riches. For some people, the temptation to get hold of these was just too great. Robbers risked their lives to steal gold, jewels and valuable objects stored deep within pyramids, and found ways to get through sealed passageways to reach the hidden burial chambers.

But it will be DARK!

ENTERING THE SECRET PASSAGE

"380, 381, 382 . . . Here we are," said Iteti, gawping up at the pyramid of Queen Neith. A quarter of the way up one of the sides, a section of stone blocks had been moved to reveal a secret entrance.

"Where are the guards?" said Nub. "Surely a royal tomb like this must be protected?"

"I think someone has bribed them to stay away," said Iteti. "Come on, we must climb and go in."

"Wait, those robbers in there are dangerous men!"

But Iteti was on her way. Reluctantly, Nub followed . . .

They found themselves in a dark passageway lit
by small oil lamps.

"This gives me the heebie-jeebies," muttered
Nub. Iteti felt her heart racing.

A stone entrance came into view. Above it were
hieroglyphs, which Nub began to read.

"It's the queen's name and . . ."

"What?" said Iteti.

"The curse."

They looked at each other. Nub gulped.
"This is the burial chamber. What shall we do?"

PUZZLES

1. The curse says, "Whoever enters this place to make evil, may the crocodile and hippopotamus take them in water, may the snake and scorpion take them on land." Why is it safe for the children to go into the tomb?

2. Nub is terrified but he decides to copy the curse to show the robbers inside the burial chamber and perhaps frighten them. The problem is that his hands are shaking. Help Nub by drawing the hieroglyphs for the word 'crocodile'. It has a meaning sign at the end. You'll need to reverse the usual codebreaking process!

CODE CLUE

Some of the sounds that were used in the ancient Egyptian language are not found in English. That's why the hieroglyph chart has four signs for 'h'. You will need to use this one:

TERROR IN THE BURIAL CHAMBER

It was a truly startling sight: a large room, adorned with paintings and gold and lit by six oil lamps, sending shadows dancing and flickering across the walls. There were richly decorated objects everywhere: beds, pots, chairs, boxes and a huge sarcophagus. Four men were so busy dropping jewellery into bags that they didn't notice the two children.

Iteti felt a blast of anger rising inside her. "Stop this!" she bellowed. Nub almost fell over in shock. "You are committing the most terrible crime of all. How dare you disturb the rest of one of Egypt's great queens?"

THE END OF THE CURSE?

Iteti and Nub hurried back through the passageway, into the blinding light. There was Senseneb, with 12 soldiers. The fleeing robbers were pinned to the ground. Behind this crowd, a sedan chair moved towards the scene, carrying the vizier himself.

"Father!" called Iteti. "I'm so glad you're here!"

"Thank the gods you're safe," he said, stepping down and embracing her. "But truly we should be thanking Senseneb for your rescue and for capturing these villains."

Nub turned to her. "What happened?"

Senseneb blushed. "I worked out some of your message, followed you, and told these guards what was going on. You two children are the bravest I have ever known."

Iteti and Nub beamed.

"The pharaoh himself will be delighted when he hears about this," smiled the vizier. "He might well consider a reward for all three of you."

"But there is another puzzle to be solved," said Senseneb. "These are just common thieves. Surely someone else must have planned this."

"I think I know who it was," said Nub.

PUZZLE

Nub wrote down his thoughts about who planned the tomb robbery. What does his message say? Is Nub right?

When they arrived back at the river there were shouts and a soldier stepped forward with another prisoner. It was Hori, the master scribe. His head was bent in shame.

"Sir, we had this man arrested after speaking with the children and your servant at the tombs," said the soldier. "Evidence shows he's the villain behind the plot."

"Excellent work," said the vizier. "But now we must see to the dead."

Queen Neith's treasure was returned to her tomb and the passageways in the pyramid filled with rubble. Her soul could rest in peace.

It had been quite an adventure, and as Nub and Iteti took one last look around, their minds were on the curse. Was it only there to scare people away, or was it real?

PUZZLES

1. Look back through the book. Can you find three clues that Hori the master scribe was involved in the tomb robberies?
2. Nub and Iteti were not sure about the power of the curse but can you find four things in this scene to suggest it might just come true?

PUZZLE SOLUTIONS

PAGE 9 – THIEVES IN THE DESERT

The Egyptian word on the papyrus scrap is **nht** which means **sycamore**.

PAGE 13 – A MARKETPLACE PLOT

The four words Nub wrote were:

- **mnfrt** (+ plural meaning sign) which means **bracelets**
- **wshnbik** which means **falcon collar**
- **shq** (+ plural meaning sign) which means **rings**
- **hne** which means **with**

So the word that is not a piece of jewellery is **hne** (with)

PAGE 17 – IN THE HOUSE OF SCRIBES

The inventory is marked below with an arrow:

PAGE 21 – A MESSAGE IN THE VIZIER'S KITCHEN

The two words are:

- **dpt** (+ boat meaning sign) which means **boat**
- **mnfyt** (+ soldier + plural meaning sign) which means **soldiers**

PAGE 22 – CROSSING THE NILE

Here is the safe route across the river:

The stowaway monkeys are circled in dark blue.

PAGE 25 – THE EMBALMING ROOMS

The evidence that the gang were in the embalming rooms is the chief robber's large hoop earring, which is lying on the floor.

PAGE 27 – THE EMBALMING ROOMS

Iteti and Nub think the thieves are planning to rob a rich person's tomb because Nub spots the word **sr** on a coffin, which means **official** (an important person).

The signs must be read from right to left!

The other hieroglyph words in the puzzle are:

- **itf** (+ male person + plural meaning signs) which means **ancestors**
- **nf** which means **those**
- **itrw** (+ water meaning sign) which means **river**
- **iqr** which means **excellent**

PAGE 29 – OBJECTS FOR THE DEAD

The robbers went through the door marked with a rhombus (diamond).

PAGE 33 – AT THE WALL OF THE GODS

The words that match the four gods (left to right) are:

- Horus – **pt** which means **sky** (+ **sky** meaning sign)
- Anubis – **mahat** which means **tomb**
- Hathor – **hbt** which means **dance** (+ **dance** meaning sign)
- Ra – **wbn** which means **shine** (+ **sunshine** meaning sign)

PAGE 34 – THE MYSTERY OF THE PYRAMIDS

The number is **382**.

PAGE 39 – ENTERING THE SECRET PASSAGE

1. It is safe for the children to enter the tomb because they are not making evil.

2. The hieroglyphs you need to draw for the word 'crocodile' are:

PAGE 43 – THE END OF THE CURSE?

The words Nub wrote were:

- **nb** which means **master** (+ male person meaning sign)
- **ss** which means **scribe** (+ male person meaning sign)
- **bin** which means **bad** (+ bad meaning sign)

So his message was 'master scribe bad'.

PAGE 45 – THE END OF THE CURSE?

1. Here are three clues that Hori the master scribe was involved in the robberies:

- He didn't help the children to solve the crime.
- The robbers had a piece of paper with hieroglyphs on at the start of the story but only scribes could write.
- Nub saw that Hori was holding a very valuable piece of jewellery, something that a noble or royal person would normally own. This was probably from a previous tomb robbery.

2. There are four clues that the curse might just come true:

- There is a scorpion behind a rock near the robbers.
- A snake can be seen by a bush near the boat.
- The boat looks like it could sink any minute (a robber mentions that his feet are getting wet). In the water nearby are 3 lurking crocodiles.
- There is also a big hippo in the water which might be aggressive.

The six cats are on pages: 10, 13, 14, 19, 20, 45.

GLOSSARY

Afterlife The life after death which ancient Egyptians believed in

Amulet An object which acts as a good luck charm

Apprentice A young person learning from a master how to do a job

Current A strong flow of water

Dates Brown fruit that grow on palm trees

Embalm To use salt or other chemicals to stop a body from rotting

Eye of Horus A sign that stood for wellness and protection

Falcon collar A large, valuable necklace in the shape of a bird

Gazelle A small, fast, deer-like animal

Hieroglyphs A way of writing using pictures and symbols to make up words and sounds

Incense A material that is burned to produce a pleasant smell

Inventory A complete list

Mummy A preserved dead body, often wrapped in bandages

Noble A rich person who rules over others

Obelisk A tall stone pillar put up at a temple or tomb

Official An official is a person in charge of something important

Palette A wooden object used to hold a scribe's ink and brushes

Papyrus Paper-like material made from reed stems

Pharaoh A king or ruler

Receipts Written notes to prove that a person bought or received something

Reed A tall grass that grows near water

River Nile The huge and very important river that flows through Egypt

Sarcophagus A stone coffin

Scarab beetle A kind of dung beetle, holy to the ancient Egyptians

Scribe A person who could read or write hieroglyphs

Scroll A rolled-up document

Shaduf A long wooden pole with a bucket hanging from one end, to collect and move water

Souls of the dead The life force of people that the ancient Egyptians thought continued after death

Sphinx A mythical creature with a human head and a lion's body

Sycamore A type of tree

Temple A large building for worship of gods

Tomb A place for burying a dead person, either underground or in a special building

Villa A large house

Vizier The most powerful person in ancient Egypt after the pharaoh